The Library of the Thirteen Colonies and the Lost Colony™

The Colony of Georgia

Brooke Coleman

The Rosen Publishing Group's
PowerKids Press™
New York

To Both My Daniels

Published in 2000 by The Rosen Publishing Group, Inc.
29 East 21st Street, New York, NY 10010

First Edition

Book Design: Andrea Levy

Coleman, Brooke.
     Georgia / by Brooke Coleman.
         p.   cm.—(The thirteen colonies and the Lost Colony series)
     Includes index.
     Summary: An introduction to the ideas that led to the colonization of the present state of Georgia in the 18th century to what life was like there for early settlers.
     ISBN 0-8239-5474-9
     1. Georgia—History—Colonial period, ca. 1600–1775—Juvenile literature. [1. Georgia—History—Colonial period, ca. 1600–1775.]
     I. Title. II. Series
     F289.C63 1999
     975.8'02—dc21   98-32371
                                                                              CIP
                                                                              AC

Manufactured in the United States of America

Contents

Before Georgia

Long before the place we call Georgia was a part of **Colonial** America, it was home to Native Americans. In the woodsy hills of northern Georgia, Cherokee Indians lived as farmers and hunters. Creek Indians had raised families for many **generations** in the hot, flat southern part of Georgia. Then many different kinds of people began to move into these Native American homelands in Georgia. First **colonists** came from Spain in the 1500s, then French and English people came in the 1600s and 1700s.

◀ *Georgia was home to several Native American tribes, then became a home for colonists.*

New Colony, New Ideas

By the early 1700s there were twelve English **colonies** in America. In 1717, a writer named Sir Robert Montgomery had an idea for a new kind of colony. He wanted it to be a **utopia**. People who had troubles in England could go there to start a new life. **Debtors** were people who couldn't pay back money they owed. Sir Robert thought these people could go to a colony in America, instead of going to jail in England. Many people read about Montgomery's ideas, but one man, James Oglethorpe, decided to turn those ideas into action.

Debtors were kept in jail until their debts were paid off. Since they couldn't make money in jail, sometimes they stayed there until they died.

The large map shows Georgia in Colonial times. ▶
The small map is a look at Georgia today.

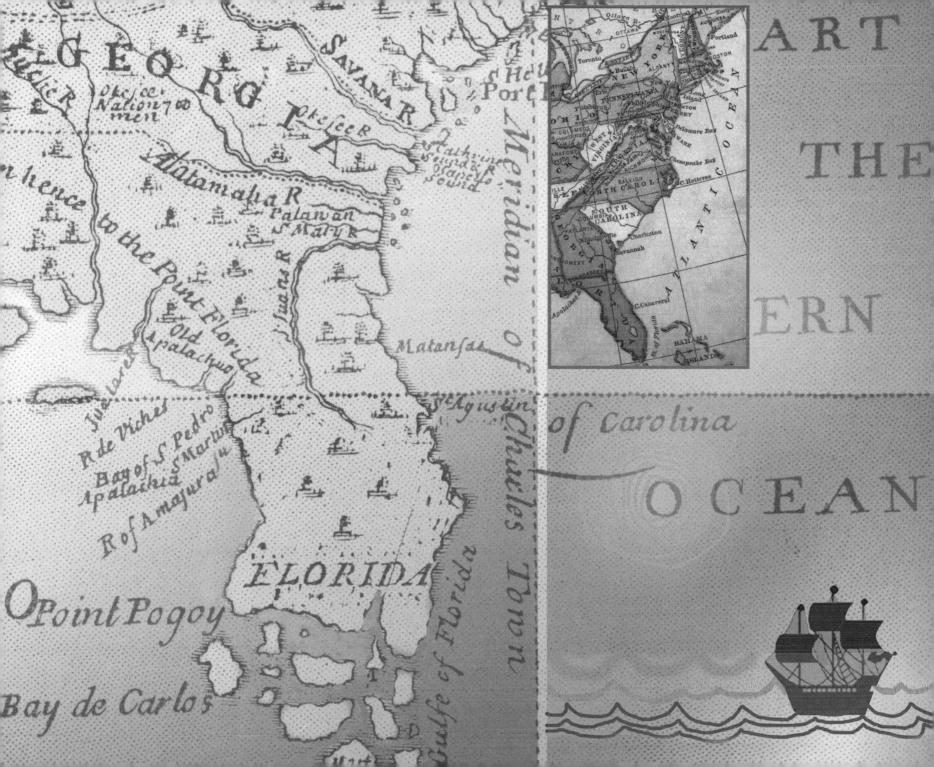

A Colony Named for a King

In 1732, King George II gave James Oglethorpe a **charter** to start his new colony. This meant that England now owned the land where Native Americans and some Spaniards had been living. The new colony was called Georgia, after King George. The charter

For over 30 years, Spain, France, and England fought over the land that would finally become Georgia.

allowed English people to settle in Georgia. The first people who came were given money to start farms. King George hoped the colonists would produce things, like wine and silk, that could be sold in England. King George also hoped the new colony would protect England's other colonies from battles with Spain.

◄ *King George hoped England could make money from Georgia's silk and wine.*

A Man with a Mission

In 1733, Oglethorpe led 114 colonists to Georgia. Some of the colonists were debtors. Other people were just looking for adventure. Oglethorpe hoped they could make Georgia the utopia that Sir Montgomery had written about. Oglethorpe made laws that were different than the laws of the other English colonies. He believed that drinking alcohol caused people to be lazy and fight each other. He made a law against buying or selling **liquor** in Georgia. Oglethorpe's laws did not let colonists own slaves. He did not think it was right for one person to own another. That law made Georgia different from all the southern colonies, and some of the northern ones.

James Oglethorpe hoped he could create a perfect place where honest people could ▶ start a new life.

The First Settlers

When Oglethorpe arrived in Georgia in 1733, he chose a beautiful place for his new town. It was near a river that flowed into the Atlantic Ocean. The colonists built the new town on a **bluff** high above this river. They called the town and the river Savannah. Oglethorpe set up Savannah, Georgia's first **capital**, very carefully. Its streets were laid out in an orderly way around a series of squares.

We're not sure how Savannah got its name. Oglethorpe might have named it after the Sawana Indians who lived nearby. It might have come from *sabana*, which is Spanish for "flat country."

◄ *The new town was built high on the riverbank to keep it safe from Indians and Spaniards who might attack.*

13

Life in Early Georgia

The colonists who came with Oglethorpe had a lot to get used to in the new land. Men, women, and children helped to build houses like the ones they had lived in back in England. The colonists also planted gardens, where they could grow food. Unfortunately, the colonists had a hard time growing many of the foods they had eaten in England. They learned to like new foods, like sweet potatoes and **maize**, which they tasted for the first time in America.

In 1752, Georgia only had 2,084 people. Today the population of Georgia is 7,055,336.

The colonists soon made the strange new land more comfortable for themselves. ▶

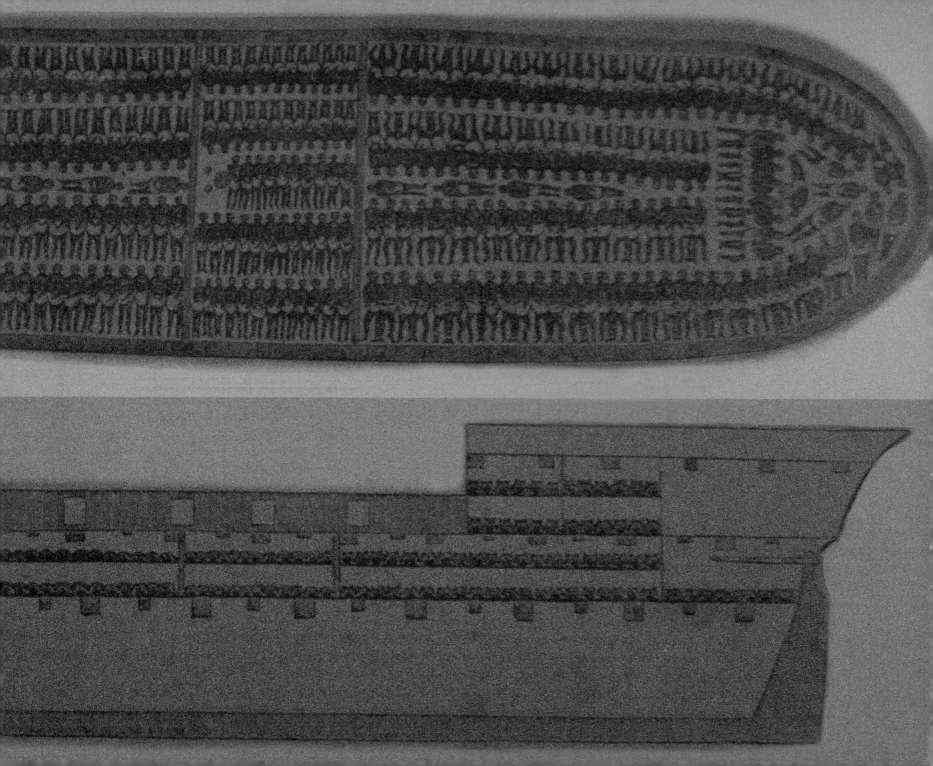

Oglethorpe's Dreams Are Lost

Most of Georgia's early colonists were **yeoman farmers**. These farmers and their families ran small farms with little help. Some colonists wanted to have big **plantations**, and they wanted slaves to do the hard work. Other Georgians wanted to change the colony's rules so that they could sell and drink alcohol. The colonists made a law in 1750, which allowed them to own slaves. Slaves were brought from Africa to work the large plantations. The colonists also began to sell and drink alcohol. Georgia was not turning out as Oglethorpe had hoped it would.

By 1752 there were 4,500 white people and 1,500 Africans in Georgia.

Africans were chained together on slave ships for the terrible three to five month trip to America.

17

The Plantation South

In 1752, Oglethorpe gave up his ideas and Georgia became a royal colony. Like most of the other colonies it was now **governed** by a royal governor, who was chosen by the king, not by the colonists. Georgia became like the other southern colonies. Big plantations took over many small farms. Although Georgia was not a good place to grow wheat, the many rivers running through flat, coastal land made it perfect for growing rice.

Georgia's small farms were replaced by huge plantations, such as this rice plantation. ▶

We the People

of the United States, in Order to form a more perfect Union, establish Justice, insure domestic Tranquility, provide for the common defence, promote the general Welfare, and secure the Blessings of Liberty to ourselves and our Posterity, do ordain and establish this Constitution for the United States of America.

Article. I.

Georgia and the Revolution

Georgia joined the other colonies when they **rebelled** against their mother country, England, in 1776. Since it was the most southern colony and easy to get to by sea, many important battles were fought in Georgia during the Revolutionary War. When the colonies won the war, America was born. Even though Georgia was the last colony started by England, it was the fourth colony to **ratify** the **United States Constitution**. Some of the **ideals** that Oglethorpe had wanted for his new colony, Georgia, became ideals that colonists wanted for their new country, the United States.

◀ *The colonists decided they wanted to make up their own rules for their new country.*

Oglethorpe Remembered

Savannah is not the capital of Georgia anymore. Georgia's modern-day capital is Atlanta, the largest city in the South, but Georgia's Colonial history and heroes are still remembered. A bronze **monument** of James Oglethorpe, founder of Savannah, has stood in Savannah's Chippewa Square since 1910. Oglethorpe and his ideas are still part of Georgia today!

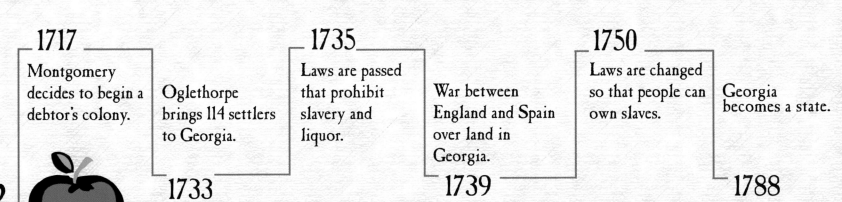

1717 Montgomery decides to begin a debtor's colony.

1733 Oglethorpe brings 114 settlers to Georgia.

1735 Laws are passed that prohibit slavery and liquor.

1739 War between England and Spain over land in Georgia.

1750 Laws are changed so that people can own slaves.

1788 Georgia becomes a state.

Glossary

bluff (BLUHF) A high, steep bank or cliff.

capital (KA-pih-tul) The place where the government for a certain area is located.

charter (CHAR-tur) An official paper giving someone permission to do something.

Colonial (kuh-LOH-nee-ul) Name for time when America was made up of thirteen colonies.

colonist (KAH-luh-nist) A person who lives in a colony.

colony (KAH-luh-nee) An area in a new country where a large group of people move, who are still ruled by the leaders and laws of their old country.

debtor (DEH-tur) A person who owes other people money.

generation (jeh-nuh-RAY-shun) The usually 20-year time between parents and birth of their children.

govern (GUH-vurn) To rule or manage.

ideals (eye-DEELZ) Beliefs about what is right.

liquor (LIH-kur) A drink that has alcohol in it.

maize (MAYZ) The Spanish word for corn.

monument (MAHN-u-mint) A statue or structure to celebrate a famous person, place, or event.

plantation (plan-TAY-shun) A very large farm where crops like tobacco and cotton were grown.

ratify (RA-tih-fy) To approve or agree to something in a formal way, like signing in public.

rebel (ruh-BEL) To disobey the people or country in charge.

United States Constitution (KAHN-stih-TOO-shun) Basic rules of the American government.

utopia (yu-TO-pee-uh) A perfect place.

yeoman farmer (YOH-men FAR-mer) A person who owns a small farm and works the farm himself.

Index

B

bluff, 13

C

capital, 13, 22
charter, 9
Cherokee Indians, 5
Colonial, 5, 22
colonies, 6, 9, 10, 17, 18, 21
colonists, 5, 9, 10, 13, 14, 17, 18, 21
Creek Indians, 5

D

debtors, 6, 10

F

founder, 22

G

generations, 5
George II, King, 9
govern, 18

I

ideals, 21

L

liquor, 10, 17

M

maize, 14
Montgomery, Sir Robert, 6, 10
monument, 22

O

Oglethorpe, James, 6, 9, 10, 13, 14, 17, 18, 21, 22

P

plantations, 17, 18

R

ratify, 21
rebel, 21

S

slaves, 10, 17

U

United States Constitution, 21
utopias, 6, 10

Y

yeoman farmers, 17

Web Sites:

You can learn more about Colonial Georgia on the Internet. Check out this Web site: http://www.cviog.uga.edu/Projects/gainfo/gahist.htm